J. J. Davey, And Others

The boy Christian

Daily Bible Studies for three Months

J. J. Davey, And Others

The boy Christian
Daily Bible Studies for three Months

ISBN/EAN: 9783337117344

Printed in Europe, USA, Canada, Australia, Japan

Cover: Foto ©ninafisch / pixelio.de

More available books at **www.hansebooks.com**

The Boy Christian

DAILY BIBLE STUDIES
FOR
THREE MONTHS

❦

COMPILED AND EDITED BY

J. J. DAVEY
J. B. CARPENTER, JR.
JAMES S. FORD
GUY C. MITCHELL
F. H. T. RITCHIE
BEN H. CAPPE

❦

NEW YORK
1899

INTRODUCTION.

THIS course of study is intended especially for the development of boys who have started in the Christian life and who are interested in Bible study. The aim in preparing the lessons has been to stimulate such boys in a daily study of God's Word for their personal growth.

It has been arranged for use :

(1) IN THE BIBLE CLASSES of the Boys' Departments of the Young Men's Christian Association. Each member of the class should have his own copy of this book and follow the outline day by day, alone, at home. In the class the teacher should review the week and emphasize such teachings as are most important to the members of the class. The course should be started so that the Seventh Day section of each week will be studied on the day of the class sessions.

(2) BY INDIVIDUAL BOYS who cannot attend such classes. Any boy may follow these studies alone. Two or three boys may undertake them together and exchange notes at the end of each week. Any point not fully understood by such boys may be submitted to the authors, who will cheerfully answer all letters concerning these studies.

This booklet is sent out with the prayer that it may be used of God in building up the spiritual lives of the boys, and in giving to workers among boys a clearer insight into the spiritual difficulties of boy-life.

Suggestions from both teachers of classes and individual boys as to the improvement of these studies will be gladly received.

Address:

J. J. DAVEY,

West Side Branch, Young Men's Christian Association,

318 West 57th Street,

New York City.

Price 10c. per copy; $1.00 per dozen.

TO BOYS

STUDY these lessons with Bible in hand, and look up each reference.

The early morning is the very best time for Bible study.

Begin each study with a prayer to God for help.

Write an answer after each question.

Do not omit to learn the Texts given.

FIRST WEEK—Sons in God's Family.

FIRST DAY.

Receiving Jesus—John 1 : 11-13.

This is the very first step in the Christian life. God offers the gift of His Son to me, and I receive the gift. The gift includes two great blessings: one is the forgiveness of my sins (Ephesians 1 : 7); the other is a *new life* which is planted within me—the kind of life Jesus would live if He were in my place (1 John 5:12).

Therefore, I will take as my motto: "What would Jesus do?" I will ask God first to tell me, and then to help me to do it.—Ephesians 3 : 20.

Question.—What would Jesus, as a boy, do in my place—at home, at school, or at work—today?

Answer.—

Text to Memorize.—John 1 : 12. "As many as received Him to them gave He power to become the sons of God, even to them that believe on His name."

FIRST WEEK—Continued.

SECOND DAY.

The Life Growing—1 Peter 2 : 1-3.

This new life has only just begun. I am like an infant and need food in order to grow. The food is the Bible. If I would do as Jesus would, I must find out from God's Word what that is.

Therefore, I will read God's Word daily and ask Him to give me some truth which shall be food for my new life.—Acts 17 : 11.

Question.—Why should I read my Bible every day?

Answer.—

Text to Memorize.—2 Peter 3 : 18. "Grow in grace, and in the knowledge of our Lord and Saviour Jesus Christ."

FIRST WEEK—Continued.

THIRD DAY.

The Life Strengthened—Matthew 6:6-13.

Now that I am a son of God, and He is to me a loving Father, He wishes me to talk with Him daily. Even if I do not feel like it, even if I feel sinful (see 1 John 1:9) and careless, He waits to have me come into the presence of His Fatherly love —Matthew 7:11.

Therefore, I will go to Him daily and ask Him for what I need.—Philippians 4:19.

Question.—What is my need to-day?

Answer.—

Text to Memorize.—Matthew 6:6. "But thou, when thou prayest, enter into thy closet, and when thou hast shut thy door, pray to thy Father which is in secret; and thy Father which seeth in secret shall reward thee openly."

FIRST WEEK—Continued.

FOURTH DAY.

The Life Guided—John 16:7-14.

Here Jesus tells His disciples how this new life is to be guided and made real to them. (See John 14:26). The Holy Spirit is to guide through the Word.

Therefore, my new life will be guided and made real to me by my remembering the words of Jesus, and by the Holy Spirit showing me the meaning.

Question.—How shall I remember the words of Jesus?—Psalm 119:15, 16.

Answer.—

Text to Memorize.—Psalm 119:105. "Thy word is a lamp unto my feet, and a light unto my path."

FIRST WEEK—Continued.

FIFTH DAY.

The Life Shown to Others—Philippians 2 : 13–16.

Now that I am a son of God, I must act as such, not murmuring nor entering into disputes, but living peaceably with those with whom I come in contact. (Romans 12 : 18.)

Therefore, if to-day I meet some boy I do not like very well, I will ask Jesus to help me to treat him right. (Galatians 6 : 10; 1 John 3 : 10.)

Question.—How would Jesus treat such a disagreeable boy as the one I have in mind?

Answer.—

Text to Memorize.—Philippians 2 : 14. "Do all things without murmurings and disputings."

FIRST WEEK—Continued.

SIXTH DAY.

The Life in Discipline—Hebrews 12 : 5-9.

Now that I am a son of God and He is my Father, He sees many things in me that need correcting, so He permits trials and troubles that I may learn lessons from them. (Hebrews 12 : 11.)

Therefore, I will thank Him even for my troubles, and ask Him what lesson He wants me to learn from them this week.

Question.—What lessons do I learn from my mistakes and troubles this week?

Answer.—

Text to Memorize.—Hebrews 12:7. "If ye endure chastening, God dealeth with you as with sons; for what son is he whom the father chasteneth not?"

FIRST WEEK — Continued.

SEVENTH DAY.

Present and Future Results of the New Life.
1 John 3: 1–5.

One of the present results of the new life is a conflict with the old life which I find still remains. In the measure to which I yield myself to Jesus the old life is overcome, and the new life is developed. (Galatians 5: 16–18.)

Therefore, I will attend to the things which will develop this new life and thus keep under the old nature. Promises to sons of God: Romans 8: 28; Ephesians 2: 10.

Question.—What are seven distinct thoughts for me as a son of God, which I have learned this week?

Answer.—

Text to Memorize.—1 John 3: 1. "Behold what manner of love the Father hath bestowed upon us that we should be called the sons of God; therefore the world knoweth us not, because it knew Him not."

SECOND WEEK—Belief, the Foundation of the New Life.

FIRST DAY.

God's Gift—John 3: 14-17.

In these verses I see that God, my Father, loved me so that He gave Jesus Christ, His only Son, in order that by simply believing I might have this new life, which is here called "eternal" and "everlasting" life.

I deserve punishment for my sin, but Jesus took my place in order that God might *rightly* give me this new life. I will read about this in 1 Peter 2: 24 and 2 Corinthians 5: 21.

Text to Memorize.—John 3: 16. "For God so loved the world that He gave His only begotten Son, that whosoever believeth in Him should not perish, but have everlasting life."

SECOND WEEK—Continued.

SECOND DAY.

The Necessity of Belief—John 3: 18-21.

The leading thought to-day is that I *must* believe with my whole heart that God sent Jesus into the world to die for my sins. If I believe, I receive new life; failing to believe, I am condemned.

See how verse 36 expresses the same thought.

Question.—What is it that abides on the unbeliever according to this verse?

Answer.—

Text to Memorize.—John 3: 18. "He that believeth on Him is not condemned; but he that believeth not is condemned already, because he hath not believed in the name of the only begotten Son of God."

SECOND WEEK—Continued.

THIRD DAY.

The Source of Belief—Romans 10: 13-17.

I have now seen that this new life is the result of what God has provided, and of my faith or belief in that provision (see John 5: 24); and to-day in the above verses I learn that this faith or belief comes by hearing the Word of God.

In Luke 8: 11, I see that the Word of God is like a seed. A seed has life and so has the Word. If I plant seed in my heart by reading the Word and let it lodge there by thinking about it, I will find that my faith or belief is strengthened; then my life will be a better life. (See Psalm 119: 9.)

Text to Memorize.—Romans 10: 17. "So then faith cometh by hearing, and hearing by the Word of God."

SECOND WEEK—Continued.

FOURTH DAY.

The Food for Belief—2 Timothy 3: 14-17.

If I stop eating food my body becomes weak; so if I neglect my new life, it also will become weak. I have learned before that the food for this new life is the Word. (See 1 Peter 2: 1-2.)

I will look up Acts 20: 32 and see what thought I get from it. I will write it out.

I see how necessary it is to think of what God's Word says. (See Jeremiah 15: 16.) What digestion is in regard to food, thinking or meditating is in regard to God's Word.

Text to Memorize.—2 Timothy 3: 16-17. "All scripture is given by inspiration of God, and is profitable for doctrine, for reproof, for correction, for instruction in righteousness: that the man of God may be perfect, thoroughly furnished unto all good works."

SECOND WEEK—Continued.

FIFTH DAY.

An Enemy of Belief.

One of the strongest enemies of belief is feeling. Read 2 Corinthians 5:7. What the Word there calls sight is the same as feeling.

Sometimes I am tempted to act as I feel, but God says I shall be happy or blessed, if I will only believe or trust. (See Proverbs 16:20.) I am to do as Abraham did. (Read Romans 4:20-22.) Whether I have feelings or not, I must believe what God says and trust His Word.

When I have no feelings with regard to my new life, I will go to God and tell Him so; but I will believe what is said in His Word, anyway.

Text to Memorize.—Romans 15:13. "Now the God of hope fill you with all joy and peace in believing, that ye may abound in hope, through the power of the Holy Ghost."

SECOND WEEK—Continued.

SIXTH DAY.

Some Results of Believing.

Look up the following passages and write after each one the result of belief there stated:

John 3: 16.

John 5: 24.

ohn 14: 12.

John 16: 27.

John 20: 31.

Question.—What shall I resolve to-day, seeing these things are so?

Answer.—

Text to Memorize.—Hebrews 12: 1, 2. "Wherefore seeing we also are compassed about with so great a cloud of witnesses, let us lay aside every weight, and the sin which doth so easily beset us, and let us run with patience the race that is set before us, looking unto Jesus the author and finisher of our faith; who for the joy that was set before him endured the cross, despising the shame, and is set down at the right hand of the throne of God."

SECOND WEEK—Continued.

SEVENTH DAY.

An Effect of Belief—1 John 3: 16–24.

True faith in Christ always produces real love for my fellows. From the fountain of the love of God to me, springs my love to Him (1 John 4: 19); and my love to Him naturally works itself out in love to my fellows. (1 John 4: 12.)

Therefore, I will to-day try to show my love to God, for what He has done for me, by loving acts and words to those whom I shall meet.

Text to Memorize.—1 John 3: 23. "And this is His commandment, that we should believe on the name of His Son Jesus Christ, and love one another, as He gave us commandment."

THIRD WEEK—Sure that I am Saved.

FIRST DAY.

The Record—1 John 5:9-13.

In the office of each county, books are kept which show who owns each piece of land in that county. If those books show a certain lot to be entered in my name, I may be sure that it lawfully belongs to me. That record is the final authority.

In the same way God has provided a record which I may consult in order to KNOW whether or not I have the Eternal Life of which I learned in the first week's study. This Record, too, is the final authority; it is the Word of God.

According to the Record, what has God given to believers? (Verse 11.)
Answer.—

Who has this Life? (Verse 12.)
Answer.—

Have I received Jesus? (See John 1:12.)
Answer.—

If so what else have I?
Answer.—

Text to Memorize.—1 John 5:11. "And this is the record, that God hath given to us eternal life, and this life is in His Son."

THIRD WEEK—Continued.

SECOND DAY.

Saved Now—John 5:24.

This is one important entry in the Record, which, as a believer, I should know by heart. I do not have to wait until some future time to KNOW that I am saved. It is my privilege to be absolutely sure of it at this moment.

"*Hath* everlasting life."

"*Is passed* from death unto life."

It does not say, I "may have" and "may pass." The "having" and the "passing" are present facts in my life from the moment when I received Jesus. I KNOW this because the Record says so, whether I have any feeling about it or not.

I will read again the verses in yesterday's study, and notice how the present tense is used: "Hath" in verses 11 and 12, and "Have" in verse 13. This life is mine NOW.

Text to Memorize.—John 5:24. "Verily, verily, I say unto you, he that heareth My Word, and believeth on Him that sent Me, hath everlasting life, and shall not come into condemnation; but is passed from death unto life."

THIRD WEEK—Continued.

THIRD DAY.

An Inward Proof—Romans 8: 14-17.

I have learned in these studies that in receiving Jesus I became a son of God. The Record has made this very plain, and because the Record says so I believe it.

Here I learn of another proof of my being a son in God's family, which comes after I have believed the Record. The Spirit of God touches my spirit, and a peace, joy, and freedom from fear, come into my heart such as were never there before.

Text to Memorize.—Romans 8: 16. "The Spirit itself beareth witness with our spirit, that we are the children of God."

THIRD WEEK—Continued.

FOURTH DAY.

Another Proof—2 Corinthians 5: 17.

When I have believed the Record, the Spirit not only gives me new peace, joy and fearlessness, but begins to change my thoughts and habits so that I may please Jesus more. I shall be more inclined to do right in all things; I shall be more loving toward those around me; I shall find more joy and help in prayer and Bible study. If I find that such changes are taking place, I may KNOW that I am a saved boy.

Text to Memorize. — 2 Corinthians 5: 17. "Therefore, if any man be in Christ, he is a new creature: old things are passed away; behold all things are become new."

THIRD WEEK—Continued.

FIFTH DAY.

Doing Right a Test—1 John 3: 4-10.

I cannot understand all that is written here, but I may get enough from it to gain some real help for my new life.

First: Verse 9 states that whosoever is a son in God's family cannot *make a practice* of sinning. "Whosoever" means me. If I have received Jesus, the Spirit will more and more make it the habit of my life to do right, and not to do wrong. If I am finding this to be so, I may KNOW that I am a saved boy.

Second: Verse 10 states that my companions know whether I belong to Jesus or to Satan, by the way I live.

Text to Memorize.—Ephesians 2: 10. "For we are His workmanship, created in Christ Jesus unto good works, which God hath before ordained that we should walk in them."

THIRD WEEK—Continued.

SIXTH DAY.

Loving Others a Test—1 John 3: 14-18.

Read also 1 John 4:7, 8. God is love, and whatever is born of God bears His likeness. The great object of my Father is to reproduce in me His own disposition and character.

The first pulse-beat of my New Life is a desire to help some other fellow. This shows that a new love has come into my life, and I stand the test mentioned in the verses of to-day. In this way I KNOW that I am a saved boy.

Text to Memorize.—1 John 4: 16. "God is love; and he that dwelleth in love dwelleth in God, and God in him."

THIRD WEEK—Continued.

SEVENTH DAY.

An Illustration—1 John 5: 11-13.

A certain farmer in the country, not having sufficient grass for his cattle, applies for a nice piece of pasture land which he hears is to be let, near his own house. For some time he gets no answer from the landlord. One day a neighbor comes in and says, "I feel quite sure you will get that field. Don't you recollect how that last Christmas he sent you a special present of game, and that he gave you a kind nod of recognition the other day when he drove past in the carriage?" And with such like words the farmer's mind is filled with sanguine hopes.

Next day another neighbor meets him, and in course of conversation he says, "I'm afraid you will stand no chance whatever of getting that grass field. Mr. —— has applied for it, and you cannot but be aware what a favorite he is with the Squire—occasionally visits with him," etc. And the poor farmer's bright hopes are dashed to the ground and burst like soap bubbles. One day he is hoping, and the next full of perplexing doubts.

Presently the postman calls and the farmer's heart beats fast as he breaks the seal of the letter, for he sees by the handwriting that it is from the Squire himself. See his countenance change from anxious suspense to undisguised joy as he reads and re-reads the letter.

"*It's a settled thing now*," exclaims he to his wife; no more doubts and fears about it;

THIRD WEEK—Continued.

"hopes" and "ifs" are things of the past. "The Squire says the field is mine as long as I require it, on the most easy terms, and *that's enough for me*. I care for no man's opinion now. *His word settles all.*"—From "Safety, Surety and Enjoyment."

> "Blessed assurance, Jesus is mine!
> O, what a foretaste of glory divine!
> Heir of salvation, purchase of God,
> Born of His Spirit, washed in His blood."

Text to Memorize.—2 Timothy 1:12. "I know whom I have believed, and am persuaded that he is able to keep that which I have committed unto him against that day."

FOURTH WEEK—Getting Rid of Sinful Habits.

FIRST DAY.

By Finding the Habits that are to be Destroyed—Colossians 3:8-10.

In these verses Paul mentions a few of the many sinful habits which are found in the natural heart (Matthew 15:19), and whose power must be broken.

Therefore, I will search my heart and see if I have any of these things within me.

Question.—What sins did I find?

Answer.—

Text to Memorize.—Colossians 3:9. "Lie not one to another, seeing that ye have put off the old man with his deeds."

FOURTH WEEK—Continued.

SECOND DAY.

By Confessing My Sins—1 John 1:6-10.

God hates the sin that is within me, and says, "The soul that sinneth, it shall die." (Ezekiel 18: 4.) By this I am condemned to death, yet God in His love for me is not willing that I should perish, and gives Jesus as a sacrifice for my sins; so that by confessing my sins and accepting the sacrifice, I am free from them.

Therefore, I will tell Him of each sin that I find in my heart, so that I may receive God's forgiveness and mercy.

Text to Memorize.—1 John 1:9. "If we confess our sins, He is faithful and just to forgive us our sins, and to cleanse us from all unrighteousness."

FOURTH WEEK—Continued.

THIRD DAY.

By Prayer—Psalm 51: 1-12.

In my prayer I must throw myself entirely upon the mercy of God. It is not by anything that I can do nor by my much speaking that God forgives me, but according to His loving kindness.

Therefore, to-day I will come in prayer to God with my burden of sin and ask Him to forgive it for Jesus' sake.

Question.—What sin do I want God to forgive to-day?

Answer.—

Text to Memorize.—Psalm 51: 10. "Create in me a clean heart, O God; and renew a right spirit within me."

FOURTH WEEK—Continued.

FOURTH DAY.

By Seeking the Right—Philippians 4:5-9.

When I have confessed my sins, I must place something in my heart in the room they left, or I will find myself in the condition of the man in Matthew 12:43-45.

Therefore, as I have forsaken my sins, and there must be something in my heart, I will think of the things that are right and pure, this day.

Question.—What have I learned in this lesson that I intend to do to-day?

Answer.—

Text to Memorize.—Philippians 4:8. "Finally, brethren, whatsoever things are true, whatsoever things are honest, whatsoever things are just, whatsoever things are pure, whatsoever things are lovely, whatsoever things are of good report; if there be any virtue, and if there be any praise, think on these things."

FOURTH WEEK—Continued.

FIFTH DAY.

By Resisting Evil—James 4: 6-8 ; 1 Peter 5: 8-9.

In the lesson to-day the thought is that I must resist evil inwardly with my spirit. If one of my boy chums should take hold of me to throw me, I would strive with all my physical power not to be thrown by him; and so inwardly I should resist with my spiritual nature the temptations of the Devil.

Therefore, according as Christ says in Matthew 26:41, I will watch and pray that I may not be taken off my guard ; thus I may be able to resist evil as soon as it appears.

Question.—In what form does evil most often come to me? Lying? disobeying? or what?

Answer.—

Text to Memorize.—James 4:7. "Submit yourselves therefore to God. Resist the devil, and he will flee from you."

FOURTH WEEK—Continued.

SIXTH DAY.

By Believing what God says about my Sins—Proverbs 6: 16-19; 1 John 2: 1, 2.

In these verses from Proverbs, I see that God hates the sins that are in me, yet in His love for me He has provided a way of escape by the life and death of His Son, Jesus Christ, who became sin for me; He, who knew no sin. (See 2 Corinthians 5: 21.)

Therefore, as God so loves me and gave His Son to deliver me from my sin, I will try and please Him by living a life like His.

Write out by the aid of the dictionary the meaning of the word "advocate."

Text to Memorize.—1 John 2: 1. "My little children, these things write I unto you, that ye sin not. And if any man sin, we have an advocate with the Father, Jesus Christ the righteous."

FOURTH WEEK—Continued.

SEVENTH DAY.

Freedom by the Truth—John 8: 31-36.

Jesus, who is the Truth, by coming into my heart makes me free from the love of sin. He breaks the power of the sinful habits that have been my masters and now I am free in Him.

Therefore, if by letting Jesus come into my heart I can gain freedom from my sinful habits, I will from this time forth surrender myself completely to Him.

Have I made a complete surrender?

Answer.—

If not, why not?

Answer.—

Text to Memorize.—John 8:32. "And ye shall know the truth, and the truth shall make you free."

FIFTH WEEK—Forming Right Habits.

FIRST DAY.

The Habit of Loving.

1 Corinthians 13: 4-8. (Revised Version.)

While breaking off bad habits, I must at the same time cultivate such habits as shall please Jesus.

"The greatest of these is love." Jesus was and is ever loving.

If I seek to know what spirit Jesus would show toward any person, I may be sure that first of all it would be love.

Therefore, I will make up my mind to be loving; to love because I *will* it, whether I feel it or not. I cannot love every one as I love my mother, but I can desire to help every one even if it costs me some sacrifice. That is the way God loves sinful men. (Romans 5:8.)

Question.—What is the name of some person toward whom I do not feel kindly, but whom I will love and help because Jesus would if He were in my place?

Answer.—

Text to Memorize.—John 15:12. "This is my commandment, that ye love one another, as I have loved you."

FIFTH WEEK—Continued.

SECOND DAY.

The Habit of Gentleness—2 Timothy 2: 24-26.

Love towards others in my heart will lead me to treat them gently. Without love I cannot be really gentle; with the love I cannot be otherwise. Jesus was a perfect gentleman, because He loved perfectly.

Therefore, I will be a true gentleman toward every one. I will speak kindly and act politely, and be as helpful as I can, with Christ's help.

Question.—What did I do yesterday that was not gentle?

Answer.—

Text to Memorize.—2 Timothy 2: 24. "The servant of the Lord must not strive; but be gentle unto all men."

FIFTH WEEK—Continued.

THIRD DAY.

The Habit of Humility—Philippians 2: 3-8.

Love towards others in my heart will lead me to think more of their good qualities and their opinions, and less of my own.

I have no reason to be boastful of my position in life, of my possessions, nor of my ability, because they are mine only as God gives them to me.

Therefore, I will not think of myself as being any better than any other fellow.

Question.—How can I carry out this intention in relation to some particular person toward whom I have acted proudly in the past?

Answer.—

Text to Memorize.—1 Peter 5: 5. "Be clothed with humility: for God resisteth the proud, and giveth grace to the humble."

FIFTH WEEK—Continued.

FOURTH DAY.

The Habit of Obedience—Ephesians 6: 1-8.

I see in these verses that real obedience begins in the heart; that I am to obey because I want to and not because I am made to do so. It is doing right when none but God sees me.

Jesus as a boy obeyed. (Luke 2:51.)

Therefore, I will make obedience a habit of my life, because it will please Jesus.

Question.—In what particular way can I obey my parents better than I have?

Answer.—

Text to Memorize.—Colossians 3:20. "Children, obey your parents in all things: for this is well pleasing unto the Lord."

FIFTH WEEK—Continued.

FIFTH DAY.

The Habit of Patience — 1 Peter 2: 18-24.

I am reminded of the patience of Jesus when He was on earth. He was conscious that He had done no wrong, and yet when reviled, persecuted and crucified, He endured without an angry word or action. This is His example to me.

Therefore, I will ask Him to help me to cultivate this habit, so that when I am misunderstood, or wrongfully accused, or asked to do what I dislike, I may not lose my temper, but be patient and long-suffering—like Jesus.

Question.—When did I last fail to be patient?

Answer.—

Text to Memorize.—1 Peter 2: 21. "Christ also suffered for us, leaving us an example, that ye should follow His steps."

FIFTH WEEK—Continued.

SIXTH DAY.

The Habit of Forgiveness—Matthew 18: 21-35.

In forgiving my sins for Christ's sake, God has cancelled a debt I never could have paid. It is beyond all calculation. Having thus forgiven me so much, He demands that I shall be very liberal in forgiving others for their smaller offenses against me. Sometimes it is hard for me to do this.

Therefore, I will ask Jesus to help me to cultivate a forgiving spirit, so that I may reflect upon others His great love and forgiveness to me. (Matthew 5: 16.)

Question.—Upon what occasion have I said I would forgive some one without meaning it?

Answer.—

Text to Memorize.—Ephesians 4: 32. "And be ye kind one to another, tender-hearted, forgiving one another, even as God for Christ's sake hath forgiven you."

FIFTH WEEK—Continued.

SEVENTH DAY.

The Habit of Thankfulness—Psalm 103.

For His gift of Jesus as my Saviour, for all His help in my life, and for His common daily blessings, I ought to be much more thankful to God than I am (James 1:17). This is another habit in which I lack.

Therefore, I will ask Jesus to help me to appreciate more fully my Father's great goodness to me, so that I shall want to thank Him more for it.

Question.—What blessing have I failed to be thankful for?

Answer.—

Text to Memorize.—Psalm 103:2. "Bless the Lord, O my soul, and forget not all His benefits."

SIXTH WEEK—The Heroic Christian.

FIRST DAY.

Heroism—Matthew 27: 26–38.

A hero, according to my idea, is one who has performed some feat of daring. The greatest hero is one who gives his life for another. (John 15: 13).

As I read these words this morning, it seems to me that Jesus fulfilled this idea in both ways. He knew what was before Him (see Luke 9: 51) but never faltered.

I wonder if I could stand the same kind of treatment, and never complain, but pray as He prayed (Luke 23: 34), "Father, forgive them, for they know not what they do."

Question.—Am I sometimes ashamed even to let my boy friends know that I believe in this great hero?

Answer.—

Question.—Am I afraid of the ridicule that would come to me if I confessed Him?

Answer.—

Prayer.—Lord Jesus, help me to be a hero in Thy cause.

SIXTH WEEK—Continued.

SECOND DAY.

Courage—Daniel 3:8-18.

To be courageous I must have a firm belief in the *cause* I serve (verses 17, 18). Foolish recklessness is not courage.

I am not likely to be cast into a fiery furnace nor to be killed for Christ's sake. There must be some other way for me to show courage. I wonder what it is? It takes *true courage* to say "No" when the boys around me say "Yes;" to stand alone for the right when others laugh and ridicule.

"You're starting, my boy, on life's journey
Along the grand highway of life;
You'll meet with a thousand temptations,
Each city with evil is rife.
This world is a stage of excitement,
There's danger wherever you go:
But if you are tempted in weakness,
Have courage, my boy, to say No!

"Be careful in choosing companions,
Seek only the brave and the true;
And stand by your friends when in trial,
Ne'er changing the old for the new;
And when by false friends you are tempted,
The taste of the wine-cup to know,
With firmness, with patience and kindness,
Have courage, my boy, to say No!"

Text to Memorize.—Psalm 27:14. "Wait on the Lord: be of good courage, and He shall strengthen thine heart."

SIXTH WEEK—Continued.

THIRD DAY.

Endurance—2 Timothy 2: 1-4.

A strong Christian life calls for the characteristics of a soldier—heroism, courage and endurance. If I follow Jesus closely, I will find there will be hard things to endure (see 2 Timothy 3: 12 and John 15: 20).

I will notice the promise in Matthew 5: 10-12.

I will see what Paul endured in 2 Corinthians 11: 23-33. How many stripes? (Verse 24.)

Answer.—

If all my boy friends should forsake me, hoot at me, refuse to play with me, throw stones at me, would I have the nerve to endure it for Christ's sake, or would I deny Christ so as to be popular with those boys?

Answer.—

"He conquers who endures."

Text to Memorize.—2 Timothy 2: 3. "Thou therefore endure hardness, as a good soldier of Jesus Christ."

SIXTH WEEK—Continued.

FOURTH DAY.

Perseverance—Luke 15: 3-10.

Here are two examples of perseverance, the shepherd sought the sheep, and the woman the coin, *until* each were found.

I am so often tempted to "give up" when difficulties come in my way. I find that the devil would have me yield to him and "give up" the things that go to make me better, for it is easier to do wrong than to do right.

I must not forget Galatians 6: 9.

Lincoln's homely maxim is a good one, "Keep pegging away."

"Keeping at it" will bring victory.

Hereafter, when I am tempted to "give up," I will try to remember and practice the text to memorize for to-day.

Text to Memorize.—1 Corinthians 15: 58. "Therefore, my beloved brethren, be ye steadfast, unmovable, always abounding in the work of the Lord, forasmuch as ye know that your labor is not in vain in the Lord."

SIXTH WEEK—Continued.

FIFTH DAY.

Self-Sacrifice—Philippians 2: 3-8.

A task difficult for anyone is to be willing to have harm come to him in order that others may be benefited by his sacrifice.

As I have read to-day, Jesus did this, and He said (Mark 10:44, 45; Luke 9:23, 24) that if I would follow Him, I must do the same.

A true hero will shun public praise, desire to put self in the back-ground, and give the credit to others.

I must forget self and disregard personal pleasure, personal indulgence, and personal advantage, when some other line of conduct is right.

In what way can I to-day sacrifice myself for others?

Answer.—

SIXTH WEEK—Continued.

SIXTH DAY.

Control—Proverbs 16: 32.

What is to be specially controlled in James 1: 26.

Answer.—

What in 1 Peter 2: 11?

Answer.—

Every sinful thought that is repressed, and every bitter word that is withheld, adds to my power with God and with man.

If I am to control my temper and my passions, God must first control my spirit. He must first govern me if I am to govern myself aright, for when I am most *fully* God-controlled, then am I most *surely* self-controlled. (See Jude 24, 25).

Text to Memorize.—1 Corinthians 6: 19, 20. "What! Know ye not that your body is the temple of the Holy Ghost, which is in you, which ye have of God, and ye are not your own? For ye are bought with a price: therefore, glorify God in your body, and in your spirit, which are God's."

SIXTH WEEK—Continued.

SEVENTH DAY.

Love—1 Corinthians 13.

The word "charity" in these verses means "*love*." I will read the chapter again and use the word "love" instead of "charity" wherever it occurs. I wonder if I cannot make out a good definition of "*love*" from these verses. Let me see.

I will write three qualities spoken of in verse 4.

Answer.—1.

2.

3.

And two in verse 5.

Answer.—1.

2.

And one in verse 6 and one in verse 7.

Answer.—1.

2.

Now if I add these things together, I find that this "*love*" is a heroic quality.

What do I find is said of it in verse 8?

Answer.—

Prayer.—"Lord Jesus, give me more of Thy love."

Text to Memorize.—1 John 4:7. "Beloved, let us love one another: for love is of God; and every one that loveth is born of God, and knoweth God."

SEVENTH WEEK—Jesus Teaching Me to Pray.

FIRST DAY.

Praying Every Day—Daniel 6: 10-23.

The passage which I have just read tells how one of God's sons talked daily with his Father, and how God blessed him. I become well acquainted with my earthly parents by talking with them every day; and I, who am God's son, will come to know my Heavenly Father in the same way.

Therefore, I will pray every day in order that I may know Him better and learn what He would have me do.

Question.—What time shall I set aside each day for talking with my Heavenly Father?

Answer.—

Text to Memorize.—Psalm 55: 17. "Evening, and morning, and at noon, will I pray, and cry aloud: and He shall hear my voice."

SEVENTH WEEK—Continued.

SECOND DAY.

Alone with God—Matthew 6:5, 6.

When I come to my Father each day, He wants me to select some quiet place where I may be alone with Him. When some one is with me, or even when my mind is full of school, work, or other things, I cannot tell Him everything freely. He wants me all alone, and He promises to give me a blessing if I go in that way.

Therefore, every day I should go away from every one, either to my own room or to some quiet place, and talk with God.

*Question.—*Will I?

Answer.—

Text to Memorize.—Matthew 6:6. "But thou, when thou prayest, enter into thy closet, and when thou hast shut thy door, pray to thy Father which is in secret; and thy Father which seeth in secret shall reward thee openly."

SEVENTH WEEK—Continued.

THIRD DAY.

Asking for a Definite Thing—Luke 18: 35-43.

Jesus asked this blind man what he wanted, and the blind man told Him. Thus Jesus teaches me to be thoughtful when I pray, and to ask for particular things.

Therefore, day by day as I come to God, I will ask Him for some definite thing for myself or for those around me.

Question.—What shall I ask from God to-day?

Answer.—

SEVENTH WEEK—Continued.

FOURTH DAY.

Sure of an Answer—Matthew 7:7-11.

Many times I grieve my Heavenly Father by not believing what He says. I know that God loves me, and that He will do what He promises. God never breaks His Word.

Therefore, each day after I have been alone with Him, and have asked Him for something, I will believe that He will answer me. It may be "yes" or it may be "no," it may come now or it may come later, as God knows best, but it is an answer just the same.

Question.—What one prayer of mine has God answered?

Answer.—

Text to Memorize.—Matthew 21:22. "All things, whatsoever ye shall ask in prayer, believing, ye shall receive."

SEVENTH WEEK—Continued.

FIFTH DAY.

One thing I must do—John 15: 1-7.

Jesus gives me a wonderful promise in the last part of verse 7, but to receive it I must do what is told me in the first part. As the branch continues to live and grow by receiving sap from the vine, so I receive my spiritual life from Christ; and when I know and obey His words (which are living words), I abide in Him and ask only for what will please Him.

Therefore, I will learn more and more of Christ's sayings and obey them.

Question.—How many of Christ's sayings can I repeat to myself in five minutes?

Answer.—

Text to Memorize.—John 15: 7. "If ye abide in Me, and My words abide in you, ye shall ask what ye will, and it shall be done unto you."

SEVENTH WEEK—Continued.

SIXTH DAY.

Always Praying—Luke 18: 1–8.

How can I be always praying? It does not mean that I am to speak aloud to God all the time, for that would be impossible. As I breathe without stopping, so should my heart always be breathing out a prayer to God.

Therefore, to-day, in the midst of all that I have to do, I will in my heart be ever thanking God for His goodness, praying for His blessing, and seeking to know His will.

Text to Memorize.—1 Thessalonians 5: 16–18. "Rejoice evermore. Pray without ceasing. In everything give thanks: for this is the will of God in Christ Jesus concerning you."

SEVENTH WEEK—Continued.

SEVENTH DAY.

Asking in Jesus' Name—John 14: 13, 14.

What a precious gift and promise! Jesus freely gives me His name to use. "To ask in the name of Jesus is to ask as if He were asking Himself."

And now, as I go daily to be alone with my Father, asking Him for definite things, abiding and trusting in Him, believing that He will surely answer me, and as I try to make my life one of continual prayer, I am to do it all in the blessed name of Jesus.

Text to Memorize.—John 16: 24. "Hitherto have ye asked nothing in my name: ask, and ye shall receive, that your joy may be full."

EIGHTH WEEK—Rules for Daily Living.

FIRST DAY.

Daily—Matthew 6: 24-34

My Father has broken up my life into days. Each day is a gift from Him. The better I use it, the less I shall have to regret when to-day becomes yesterday.

> "Build a little fence of trust
>   All around to-day;
> Fill it in with loving deeds
>   And within it stay.
> Look not through its sheltering bars
>   Out upon to-morrow.
> God will keep whatever comes,
>   Be it joy or sorrow."

> "Moment by moment I'm kept in His love,
> Moment by moment I've life from above,
> Looking to Jesus till glory doth shine,
> Moment by moment, O Lord, I am Thine."

See Isaiah 27: 3.

Text to Memorize.—Deuteronomy 33: 25. "As thy days, so shall thy strength be."

EIGHTH WEEK—Continued.

SECOND DAY.

Daily Prayer—Psalm 55: 16, 17.

David went to God in prayer three times a day. Jesus himself prayed often (see Mark 1:35; Luke 5:16, 9:29). How much more necessary is it for me to pray daily, that I may be able to live a Christlike life.

Therefore, I will let no day pass without doing so.

Question.—Do I really pray, or simply "say my prayers"?

Answer.—

Text to Memorize.—Matthew 7:7. "Ask, and it shall be given you ; seek, and ye shall find ; knock, and it shall be opened unto you."

EIGHTH WEEK—Continued.

THIRD DAY.

Daily Bible Study—Acts 17: 10-12.

Here I see why the early Christians in Berea were more noble than those in Thessalonica. If I would be noble, I, too, must study His Word. This is one of the ways my Father talks to me and tells me how He would have me live.

Question.—What results of Bible study do I find in 2 Timothy 2: 15?

Answer.—1.

2.

Text to Memorize.—Luke 11:28. "Yea, rather, blessed are they that hear the Word of God and keep it."

EIGHTH WEEK—Continued.

FOURTH DAY.

Daily Dependence—Psalms 70: 4, 5 and 71: 1-3.

In His loving desire to keep me close to Himself, my Father sends into my life each day certain needs which I alone am unable to supply. This leads me to depend upon Him, rather than upon myself.

" I need Thee every hour, stay Thou near by ;
Temptations lose their power, when Thou art nigh.

I need Thee every hour, teach me Thy will,
And Thy rich promises in me fulfill."

I need Thee, oh ! I need Thee,
Every hour I need Thee ;
O, bless me now, my Saviour ! I come to Thee.

Text to Memorize.—Philippians 4: 19. "But my God shall supply all your need according to His riches in glory by Christ Jesus."

EIGHTH WEEK—Continued.

FIFTH DAY.

Daily Self-Denial—Matthew 20: 28; John 6: 38; Romans 15: 3; Philippians 2: 6–8.

Christ is my great example in self-denial. I see in the readings of to-day that He denied Himself the things of this world in order that He might be able to do His Father's will.

In Romans 12: 1, 2, I am asked to do the same.

Question.—Am I willing?

Answer.—

EIGHTH WEEK—Continued.

SIXTH DAY.

Daily Obedience.

Obedience is hard sometimes. God knows that hard things are good for me; that is one reason why He demands them.

God teaches me in His word that obedience is due both to Him and to my parents. Let me see what I can learn about it to-day.

> Due to God—Deuteronomy 13:4; Acts 5:29.
>
> Due to Parents—Ephesians 6:1–3; Colossians 3:20.
>
> Result of Obedience to God—Deuteronomy 11:26–28.

I find an example of the result of obedience in Luke 5:4–6. Obedience to Jesus turns failure into success.

Question.— Will I make up my mind to obey Him, not only when I feel so inclined, but daily?

Answer.—

EIGHTH WEEK—Continued.

SEVENTH DAY.

Daily Serving—Romans 12: 1-21.

"What this world needs is sermons in shoes."
—*Cuyler*.

"Actions speak louder than words."

"What you *are* thunders so loud in my ears that I cannot hear what you *say*."

I may not be able to preach in words; but a Christlike life is a daily sermon.

Question.—What am I going to do about it?

Answer.—

Text to Memorize.—Matthew 5: 16. "Let your light so shine before men, that they may see your good works, and glorify your Father which is in heaven."

NINTH WEEK—Seeking Best Things First.

FIRST DAY.

First—1 Kings 3:5-14.

To-day's reading is an illustration of Matthew 6:33.

Bible study and prayer are the mediums through which the *first things* of God are known. God wants me to put these first things first each day, so that I shall be strengthened to discern good and evil. Each morning Satan tries to insert a postponement of these things as an opening wedge, because he knows that by such neglect my spiritual senses will be made dull.

God comes to me and asks, "My boy, what shall I give you?" Shall I say to Him, "Give me riches, long life, and prosperity, first, and then I will serve Thee;" or will I say with Solomon, "Lord, give me a heart that can tell good from evil?"

NINTH WEEK—Continued.

SECOND DAY.

God's Kingdom—Matthew 6: 19-34.

What do I suppose the Kingdom of God really is? Do I think it is heaven? It is not exactly that. It is letting Christ live in my heart and rule it. The kingdom of England consists not of the land but of every man who is an Englishman, wherever he may be living, and so it is with the Kingdom of God.

Therefore, I am a part of the Kingdom of God, because Christ is my King, and I am letting Him rule in my life.

Question.—In what one thing to-day may I show my loyalty to my King?

Answer.—

Text to Memorize.—Matthew 6: 33. "But seek ye first the Kingdom of God, and His righteousness; and all these things shall be added unto you."

NINTH WEEK—Continued.

THIRD DAY.

My Father—Isaiah 55: 6-11.

I notice that the seventh verse tells me how to fulfill the sixth verse. I see also how James 4: 8 suggests the same way of drawing near to my Father.

What separates me from Him? (Isaiah 59: 2.)

Answer.—

What must I do with sin in order to draw near to my Father?

Answer.—

Therefore, shall I not to-day put into practice the commands of Isaiah 55: 6, 7, and as a result find—what? (2 Corinthians 6: 17, 18.)

Answer.—

Text to Memorize.—Isaiah 55: 6. "Seek ye the Lord while He may be found, call ye upon Him while He is near."

NINTH WEEK—Continued.

FOURTH DAY.

His Strength—Psalm 46.

Good morning! If I tried what was said yesterday, I know how much better the day went. But here is something more. I will look at that first verse. God has abundant strength and power, and has promised to supply my need of the same. (Philippians 4: 19.)

Therefore, in my weakness I will ask my Father for His strength.

Question.—For what weakness of mine will I to-day seek God's strength?

Answer.—

Text to Memorize.—Psalm 46: 1 (Luther's favorite Psalm). "God is our refuge and strength, a very present help in trouble."

NINTH WEEK—Continued.

FIFTH DAY.

His Teachings—Psalm 119:41-48.

One of the best things that God would have me seek is in the forty-fifth verse:—His precepts, or, in other words, His teachings. I notice that it says that "I will walk at liberty" when I do this.

Have I found myself happier since I have looked into God's own Word for His teachings? I will keep on looking!

In the light of this, I will hide in my heart as much of His Word as I can (Psalm 119:11), and then I will know what He wants me to do.

If this is such liberty, why keep it all to myself? Verse 46 speaks of testifying before kings. If I don't know any kings, I do know some boy. Why not get him to seek God's teaching?

Question.—Who?

Answer.—

Text to Memorize.—Psalm 119:105. "Thy Word is a lamp unto my feet, and a light unto my path."

NINTH WEEK—Continued.

SIXTH DAY.

His Will—Hebrews 13: 20, 21.

The very highest point in the Christian life is mentioned in these two verses. Read them over again. *To do God's will!* There was only one who ever did it perfectly.

Question.—Who was that? (John 8: 29.)

Answer.—

I will this morning find what are some of the things God wills that I should do. God's will is revealed in His Word, so I will look there for my knowledge.

Question.—What is said to be God's will in the following verses:

(*a*) 1 Peter 2: 15?

Answer.—

If I let Christ live in the whole of my life, people will know I am a Christian.

(*b*) 1 Peter 2: 20?

Answer.—

This is meant for me. I can ask myself, "What would Jesus do?"

(Concluded on next page)

NINTH WEEK—Continued.

SIXTH DAY—Concluded.

(*c*) 1 Thessalonians 5: 18?

Answer.—

In my home am I giving thanks or finding fault?

Text to Memorize.—Philippians 2: 13. "For it is God which worketh in you both to will and to do of His good pleasure."

NINTH WEEK—Continued.

SEVENTH DAY.

Results.

In the blank spaces write the omitted words of the following scriptures :

Psalm 34: 10. "They that seek the Lord shall —— —— —— —— ——."

Proverbs 3: 5, 6. "Trust in the Lord with all thine heart ; and lean not unto thine own understanding. In all thy ways acknowledge Him and He shall —— —— —— ——."

Psalm 37: 3, 4. "Trust in the Lord and do good ; so shalt thou —— —— —— ——, and verily thou shalt —— ——. Delight thyself also in the Lord, and He shall —— —— —— —— —— —— ——."

Romans 8: 28. "And we know that —— —— —— —— —— to them that love God, to them who are the called according to His purpose."

Count your blessings.

Text to Memorize.—Jeremiah 29: 13. "And ye shall seek Me, and find Me, when ye shall search for Me with all your heart."

TENTH WEEK—Sowing and Reaping.

FIRST DAY.

Sowing—Galatians 6: 1-10.

Satan is a great deceiver. (Revelation 12: 9.) God wants us to know the truth. I notice especially that seventh verse. Everything I say and everything I do is seed—good or bad. Whether conscious of it or not, I am always *sowing*, and my life is a constant invitation for other fellows to do as I do.

> "Sowing the seed by the daylight fair,
> Sowing the seed by the noon-day glare,
> Sowing the seed by the fading light,
> Sowing the seed in the solemn night;
> Oh! What will the harvest be?"

Seeing that these things are so, I will to-day think upon, and put into practice, Psalm 119: 9-11.

Text to Memorize.—Psalm 119: 9. "Wherewithal shall a young man cleanse his way? by taking heed thereto according to Thy Word."

TENTH WEEK—Continued.

SECOND DAY.

Reaping—Galatians 6: 1–10.

I cannot sow thistles and reap wheat.

I cannot sow bad thoughts and keep a clean mind.

I cannot do a bad act and reap good results (verse 7).

My Father is absolutely just and is no respecter of persons. (See Acts 10: 34, and Romans 2: 6.)

> "Sow a thought, reap an act;
> Sow an act, reap a habit;
> Sow a habit, reap a character;
> Sow a character, reap a destiny."

Text to Memorize.—Galatians 6:7. "Be not deceived; God is not mocked: for whatsoever a man soweth, that shall he also reap."

TENTH WEEK—Continued.

THIRD DAY.

Good Seed—Philippians 4:8.

All that is mentioned in this verse may be called good seed. Throughout the Bible there are many other references to the same things, sometimes in other words.

Which of the things in this passage do I find in :

Proverbs 12: 17?

Hebrews 13: 18?

1 Timothy 5: 22?

The seed I am now sowing is for the whole of life. Every action of mine is counted and registered in the nerve cells and fibres of my body. If repeated, the action is stamped forever on my life.

TENTH WEEK—Continued.

FOURTH DAY.

Bad Seed—Matthew 7: 16-20.

A repeated act has the strange power of getting itself repeated again and again. A boy becomes a slave to his constantly repeated acts whether they be good or bad.

One of the best ways of keeping the bad seed out of my life is to keep busy sowing good seed. See Romans 12: 21.

If I sow bad seed of any kind "just to see what it is like," I shall surely reap a bad harvest.

Question.—What bad seed have I been sowing this last week, which I will now confess and forsake?

Answer.—

Text to Memorize.—Romans 12: 21. "Be not overcome of evil, but overcome evil with good."

TENTH WEEK—Continued.

FIFTH DAY.

Good Seed Growing—Mark 4: 26-29.

These verses show me that I do not always reap *at once* that which I sow. It takes time for good seed to grow and develop. I must be patient if it seems to grow slowly. See Galatians 6: 9.

The Word of God is full of good seed; and if I am faithfully planting it in my mind, it will surely bring forth fruit because of the promise in Isaiah 55: 10, 11.

Text to Memorize.—Galatians 6: 9. "And let us not be weary in well doing: for in due season we shall reap, if we faint not."

TENTH WEEK—Continued.

SIXTH DAY.

Bad Seed Growing—Luke 8:7.

Weeds seem to grow more quickly than good plants, and ofttimes bad deeds seem to develop more rapidly than good ones.

What bad seeds am I warned against in :

Ecclesiastes 7: 9?

2 Timothy 3: 2?

1 Peter 2: 11?

Text to Memorize.—1 Timothy 4:12. "Let no man despise thy youth; but be thou an example of the believers, in word, in conversation, in charity, in spirit, in faith, in purity."

TENTH WEEK—Continued.

SEVENTH DAY.

Sowing and Reaping.

Write out below the answers found in the texts.

What?
  Mark 4: 14 :

  Luke 8: 11 :

  1 Peter 1: 23 :

When?
  2 Timothy 4: 2 :

  Ecclesiastes 11: 6 :

Where?
  Matthew 13: 4-8 (Four places) :

How?
  2 Corinthians 9: 6 :

  Proverbs 11: 24 :

  John 15: 5 :

Result?
  Proverbs 11: 18 :

ELEVENTH WEEK—Temptation.

FIRST DAY.

The Temptation of Jesus—Matthew 4: 1-11.

Notice carefully in the first verse, (*a*) by whom He was tempted; and (*b*) by whom He was led to the temptation.

In how many ways was He tempted? (Verses 3, 5, 8.)

Answer.—

What same three words did Jesus use in each of His replies to Satan? (Verses 4, 7, 10.)

Answer.—

How was Jesus helped after He resisted Satan? (Verse 11.)

Answer.—

What is told me about Jesus in the last clause of Hebrews 4: 15?

Answer.—

Why is it very helpful for me to know that Jesus was tempted? (Hebrews 2: 18).

Answer.—

Text to Memorize.—Hebrews 2: 18. "For in that He Himself hath suffered being tempted, He is able to succor them that are tempted."

ELEVENTH WEEK—Continued.

SECOND DAY.

The Tempter—Job 1:6-12.

This tells me of the temptation of another good man, Job. Satan is represented as saying that Job trusted God only because God had made him prosperous, and that he would sin if God took away his property and comfort.

In order to prove the reality of Job's trust in God, God gave Satan permission to tempt Job; first, by taking away all his possessions, and afterward (chapter 2:6) by afflicting his body in any way, if only he spared his life.

Notice that Satan can tempt only as God permits.

What name of the tempter is used in this study?

Answer.—

What other name was used in yesterday's study?

Answer.—

Who never tempts any man? (James 1:13.)

Answer.—

Text to Memorize.—2 Peter 2:9. "The Lord knoweth how to deliver the godly out of temptations."

ELEVENTH WEEK—Continued.

THIRD DAY.

Who are Tempted, and When?
Luke 22: 31-34; 54-62.

Who was tempted in the first lesson this week?

Answer.—

Who in yesterday's lesson?

Answer.—

Who in to-day's lesson?

Answer.—

Satan spares no one. Some think that good men are not tempted. Some boys think that after they become Christians, they will be free from temptation and sin.

I am learning this week that such is not the case. Jesus was tempted immediately after His baptism. Job, with others, was in God's presence for worship. Peter had promised always to be faithful to Jesus.

Those who live closest to Jesus are the ones whom Satan tries hardest to tempt into sin. When any one starts out to serve Christ, or to do anything else that is right, then Satan makes a special effort to prevent his doing so.

Text to Memorize.—1 Peter 5: 8. "Be sober, be vigilant, because your adversary the devil, as a roaring lion, walketh about, seeking whom he may devour."

ELEVENTH WEEK—Continued.

FOURTH DAY.

How Satan Tempts—Mark 7:20-23.

All temptation comes from Satan, but each person is tempted in different ways and to a greater or less extent.

I *think* of evil things before I *do* them (Proverbs 23:7); so Satan uses many means by which to suggest bad thoughts to my mind.

Some temptations are entirely from within myself. They are the work of Satan through my sinful nature. Such, for instance, are the temptations to be selfish and to be impure.

Other temptations come from outside influences. Satan uses the evil that is without to excite the evil that is within me. Looking at bad pictures, reading bad books, hearing bad stories, are examples.

Sometimes Satan leads other boys, or wicked men, to teach me bad habits and lead me to sin. (Proverbs 1:10.)

Text to Memorize.—Psalms 51:10. "Create in me a clean heart, O God; and renew a right spirit within me."

ELEVENTH WEEK—Continued.

FIFTH DAY.

Temptation is Not Sin—Job 2:6-10.

Did Jesus sin when He was tempted? (See Hebrews 4:15.)

Answer.—

Did Job? (See Job 1:22.)

Answer.—

I cannot keep Satan from knocking at my door, but I need not invite him to enter. Some one may ask me to steal (that would be a temptation), but if I turn away from him I do not sin. I may have an evil thought. If I immediately put away that thought and begin to think of something good, I have been tempted, but I have not sinned. If I let the evil thought stay in my mind and grow there, then I sin, and probably I will soon *do* something wrong as a result of the evil thinking.

If I say "yes" to a temptation, it becomes sin; if I say "no," it does not.

Text to Memorize.—1 Corinthians 10:13. "There hath no temptation taken you but such as is common to man: but God is faithful, who will not suffer you to be tempted above that ye are able; but will with the temptation also make a way to escape, that ye may be able to bear it."

ELEVENTH WEEK—Continued.

SIXTH DAY.

How to Meet Temptation—Ephesians 6: 10-18.

In the eighteenth verse I have the secret of success in this matter. What similar teaching did Jesus give us in Matthew 26: 41?

Answer.—

What is said about the tempter in James 4: 7?

Answer.—

"Resist" is a strong word. Handling temptations lightly will not resist them. I must act earnestly. The resistance that will succeed consists of the two parts, prayer and watchfulness.

Human strength cannot win against spiritual enemies. I must have spiritual help, and so I must commit my weak point to God every day for Him to keep. I must *pray* as if all depended on God.

Then I must *watch* as if all depended on myself, and keep away from every influence which might lead me into sin.

Text to Memorize.—Romans 12: 21. "Be not overcome of evil, but overcome evil with good."

ELEVENTH WEEK—Continued.

SEVENTH DAY.

Why I am Tempted—James 1: 2-4.

Temptation is a proof of God's love. He permits me to be tempted, not because He wants me to sin, but in order that I may become strong in my Christian life through testing.

Silver is not good for use in its natural state. It must be tried in the fire that the dross may be taken out and the metal purified. So God deals with His children whom He loves so much.

When I am tempted I will remember this.

Text to Memorize.—James 1: 12. "Blessed is the man that endureth temptation: for when he is tried, he shall receive the crown of life, which the Lord hath promised to them that love him."

TWELFTH WEEK—My Relationships to God.

FIRST DAY.

A Son—1 John 3: 1-3.

I learned in the first week's study that I, as a believer, had already received a place as a son in God's family. It is hard for me to realize that this is so. If I did realize it, I would act differently.

Think of it! God's son! A son of Him who made the heavens and the earth. Psalm 8: 3-9. A son of Him who cares even for a sparrow. Matthew 10: 29-31.

What does 1 John 3: 1 say is my relation to this world, as God's son?

Answer.—

Text to Memorize.—1 John 3:1. "Behold, what manner of love the Father hath bestowed upon us, that we should be called the sons of God: therefore the world knoweth us not, because it knew Him not."

TWELFTH WEEK—Continued.

SECOND DAY.

An Heir—Galatians 4:6, 7.

As a son in God's family, I have my Father's loving care and protection. As an heir, I inherit His possessions. I have different needs, and as an heir I can ask Him to supply them. Philippians 4:19.

"My Father is rich in houses and lands,
He holdeth the wealth of the world in His hands;
Of rubies and diamonds, of silver and gold,
His coffers are full; He hath riches untold.

"I once was an outcast stranger on earth,
A sinner by choice, an alien by birth;
But I've been adopted, my name's written down,
An heir to a mansion, a robe, and a crown!"

Text to Memorize.—Galatians 4:6. "And because ye are sons, God hath sent forth the Spirit of His Son into your hearts, crying, Abba, Father."

TWELFTH WEEK—Continued.

THIRD DAY.

A Child—Romans 8: 14-17.

Danger ahead! These two lessons may have made me feel big, so to-day I must remember that I am a child. My parents give me certain privileges which they consider best for me, and when I step over the boundary of these privileges they check me. So with God ; He knows what is good for me and lets me enjoy the riches as He sees best.

I see that a son must not use the riches for himself alone. Others must be considered in using my inheritance.

Text to Memorize.—Romans 8: 16. "The Spirit itself beareth witness with our spirit, that we are the children of God."

TWELFTH WEEK—Continued.

FOURTH DAY.

A Special Boy—Deuteronomy 7:6-8; Titus 2:14.

God has adopted me as a son, not simply that I may enjoy and spend His gifts. He has a plan for me. I am to be a specialist in giving out to others the good I receive from Him. This often means winning some other boy to Christ. I am to be zealous and earnest in working out His plan for me, not half-hearted or careless.

To be a special boy, one that can glorify God, I do not have to put on a long face and assume a holy voice for the occasion. I am to be my real self, joyful, happy, living in God's sunlight, always earnest in God's work.

Text to Memorize.—Titus 2: 14. "Who gave Himself for us, that He might redeem us from all iniquity, and purify unto Himself a peculiar people, zealous of good works."

TWELFTH WEEK—Continued.

FIFTH DAY.

A Holy Temple.
1 Corinthians 3: 16, 17; 6: 19-20.

Just as the Jews of old kept and repaired their temple where God talked to them, so to-day God wants me to keep my body clean and healthy, a fit place for Him to dwell in.

My! these are strange words. I wonder if those angry words which I spoke yesterday hurt my body. I was thinking of smoking to-day, but I think now I would better not; it would soil the temple of God. I wonder if that secret sin that only God sees, is hurting my body. Oh, how clean I must be in thought, in word, and in deed, to have a temple fit for God to live in.

Text to Memorize.—1 Corinthians 6: 20. "For ye are bought with a price; therefore glorify God in your body, and in your spirit, which are God's."

TWELFTH WEEK—Continued.

SIXTH DAY.

A Royal Priest—1 Peter 2: 1-10.

A priest in the olden time was a man who stood between God and man. He offered sacrifices for the sins of the people. Christ became my high priest and gave Himself as the sacrifice. I accept Christ and I am then made a priest—a boy to save boys. How? By my prayers, my works of love, and my life in Christ, I stand between God and the unsaved boy.

This is a great responsibility. I have obtained mercy from God, and now I must help other boys to obtain this same mercy from Him, or I shall fail in my life.

I am a priest. God help me to fulfill my office aright.

Text to Memorize.—1 Peter 2:9. "But ye are a chosen generation, a royal priesthood, an holy nation, a peculiar people; that ye should shew forth the praises of Him, who hath called you out of darkness into His marvelous light."

TWELFTH WEEK—Continued.

SEVENTH DAY.

A Co-Worker—1 Corinthians 3:9.

It is a great privilege to be called a son, an heir, and a child, of God; to have my body honored as the dwelling-place of God; to be installed in the office of priesthood; yet more wonderful is it to know that I am so loved and honored by Him that He makes me a co-worker with Himself, makes me His partner in working out His plans for saving the world from sin. Partners are most successful when they are most constant and intimate in their relationship. Read John 15:15, 16 and see the same thought expressed differently.

Text to Memorize.—1 Corinthians 3:9. "For we are laborers together with God: ye are God's husbandry, ye are God's building."

THIRTEENTH WEEK—Power.

FIRST DAY.

What is it?—Acts 1:6-8.

What is the power spoken of in verse 8?

It is called the power of the Holy Spirit (Romans 15:13) and is the presence of the life of God within my life.

Like the power of electricity, I cannot see nor fully explain this power, but I know it exists: because it has been seen to work through the lives of men ever since Christ left this earth. John 16:7.

Who had this power in Acts 4:8?

Answer.—

Who in Acts 13:9?

Answer.—

THIRTEENTH WEEK—Continued.

SECOND DAY.

Is it for me?—Acts 2: 37-39.

The promise spoken of in verse 39 refers to the gift mentioned in verse 38.

The Spirit of power was given to Jesus for His own life work. Matthew 3: 16-17.

He wants my life work to be like His (see John 14: 12), and He went away so as to send the same power upon me for this work (see John 16:7).

To-day's reading shows this power to be possible to all who have forsaken their sins and received Jesus as their Savior.

Have I received Jesus?

Answer.—

May I have this power?

Answer.—

THIRTEENTH WEEK—Continued.

THIRD DAY.

How do I get it?

In the first lesson I saw that there was such a thing as power from God, and in the second lesson I saw that it was for me. To-day I must find out how I receive it.

As I received forgiveness, so also do I receive this power—by *faith* in Christ (see Galatians 3: 14).

I find, according to Luke 11:13, that I receive this gift by *asking*.

In Acts 8: 18-23, I see that I must *forsake* all known sin.

In Acts 5: 32, I learn that I must *obey* without hesitation.

I will write down these four things which I must do in order to receive this gift.

1.

2.

3.

4.

THIRTEENTH WEEK—Continued.

FOURTH DAY.

What hinders it?—Ephesians 4: 20-32.

God will not put His power into unclean instruments.

What are some of the things that hinder?

In verse 22?

" " 25?

" " 28?

" " 29?

" " 31? (1)

(2)

(3)

(4)

(5)

Read 2 Timothy 2: 21.

THIRTEENTH WEEK—Continued.

FIFTH DAY.

What will be its Chief Result in my Life?
Galatians 5: 22-26.

In the reading to-day I see that the chief quality of the Spirit is love.

The other qualities mentioned in verses 22 and 23 show that the love exists.

When the Spirit enters into my life, His first work is to shed abroad the love of God in my heart. (Romans 5: 5.)

It is the love of God taking up abode within me. (John 17: 26.)

Therefore, the chief result will be that *love* will become the keynote of my life, and I shall be joyous, peaceful, long-suffering, gentle, good, faithful, meek, and temperate in all things.

THIRTEENTH WEEK—Continued.

SIXTH DAY.

How will it Affect Other Lives through me?
Luke 4:16-19.

Jesus had the Spirit upon His life in order that He might be a blessing to others. God will give me this same power for the same purpose.

This is God's plan for my life (see Ephesians 2:10).

I am commanded to be "filled with the Spirit" (Ephesians 5:18), and to the extent to which I obey this command will God work in and through me to help others to live a more Christlike life.

THIRTEENTH WEEK—Continued.

SEVENTH DAY.

Shall I Yield Myself to it?—Romans 6: 12-16.

Two powers want to occupy my body. One is Christ through the Holy Spirit, the other is Satan. I must yield to one or the other. (Matthew 6: 24.)

Which shall it be? Read Romans 12: 1-2.

Answer.—

Knowing what this power is, (First day);

Knowing that it is possible for me to have it, (Second day);

Knowing how I may get it, (Third day);

Knowing what will hinder my having it, (Fourth day);

Knowing how it will uplift and ennoble my own life, (Fifth day);

Knowing how helpful it will make me to others, (Sixth day);

AM I WILLING TO-DAY TO YIELD MYSELF?

Answer.—

Luke 24: 49 (Revised Version)—"Tarry until ye be clothed with power from on high."

Revelation 4: 2.—"And immediately I was in the Spirit."

INDEX.

WEEK.	TOPIC.	PAGE.
1	Sons in God's Family	7
2	Belief, the Foundation of the New Life	14
3	Sure that I am Saved	21
4	Getting Rid of Sinful Habits	29
5	Forming Right Habits	36
6	The Heroic Christian	43
7	Jesus Teaching Me to Pray	50
8	Rules for Daily Living	57
9	Seeking Best Things First	64
10	Sowing and Reaping	72
11	Temptation	79
12	My Relationships to God	86
13	Power	93

www.ingramcontent.com/pod-product-compliance
Lightning Source LLC
Chambersburg PA
CBHW020900160426
43192CB00007B/1002